EXPLORE A CAVE

BY K.C. KELLEY

AMICUS READERS ● AMICUS INK

amicus readers

Amicus Readers and Amicus Ink are imprints of Amicus
P.O. Box 227, Mankato, MN 56002
www.amicuspublishing.us

Names: Kelley, K. C., author.
Title: Explore a cave / by K.C. Kelley.
Description: Mankato, MN : Amicus, [2018] | Series: Amazing adventures
Identifiers: LCCN 2017022593 (print) | LCCN 2017054831 (ebook) | ISBN 9781681513508 (pdf) | ISBN 9781681513140 (library binding : alk. paper) | ISBN 9781681522708 (pbk. : alk. paper)
Subjects: LCSH: Caves--Juvenile literature.
Classification: LCC GB601.2 (ebook) | LCC GB601.2 .K45 2018 (print) | DDC 551.44/7--dc23
LC record available at https://lccn.loc.gov/2017022593

Editor: Marysa Storm/Megan Peterson
Designer: Patty Kelley
Photo Researcher/Producer: Shoreline Publishing Group LLC

Photo Credits: Cover: Salajean/Dreamstime.com
Dreamstime.com: Martingraf 9; Mario Madrona Barrera 16R; insider2D 16B ; iStock.com: Aaron Choi 11; Senckenberg Research Institute: 16T; Shutterstock: Waldru 3; Natalia Maroz 4; triocean 13; Hanoi Photography 15; USGS National Wildlife Health Center: 6.

Sophie spots a big hole.
Or is it a cave?

Caves are underground or inside rocks. They can be very deep.

PETZL
Black Dia

Animals live in caves. Joe looks at some bats.

The air in caves is cool. Some caves have rivers or lakes.

Some caves
are very big.
A crowd fits
in this one.
What do they see?

Cave rocks have odd shapes. Jack likes the pointy ones! They are called stalactites.

There's the sun.
We're almost out!

CAVE ANIMALS

cave spider

bat

cave frog